KU-484-321

# Avalanches

Michele Ingber Drohan

The Rosen Publishing Group's
**PowerKids Press**™
New York

For Morgan Ashley

Published in 1999 by The Rosen Publishing Group, Inc.
29 East 21st Street, New York, NY 10010

Copyright © 1999 by The Rosen Publishing Group, Inc.

First Edition

Book Design: Danielle Primiceri

Photo Credits: pp. 5, 6, 9, 10, 14, 17, 18 © Patrick Cone Photography; pp. 13, 21 © Galen Rowell/Mountain Light Photography Inc.

Drohan, Michele Ingber.
    Avalanches / by Michele Ingber Drohan.
        p.    cm.— (Natural disasters)
    Includes index.
    Summary: Discusses how different types of avalanches are caused, how they may be prevented, and how people can protect themselves and their homes from this type of disaster.
    ISBN  0-8239-5283-5
    1. Avalanches—Juvenile literature. [1. Avalanches.]  I. Title. II. Series: Drohan, Michele Ingber.  Natural disasters.
    QC929.A8D76  1998
    551.57'848—dc21
                                                                                    98-15379
                                                                                    · CIP
                                                                                    AC

Manufactured in the United States of America

# Contents

# Snow

Did you know that snow is made of many different ice **crystals** (KRIS-tulz)? Ice crystals form when water **vapor** (VAY-per) in the air freezes. These crystals come together around a dust **particle** (PAR-tih-kul). As more crystals come together, the clump gets heavy. When it grows heavy enough, the group of crystals falls from the sky. This group of ice crystals is called a snowflake. As a snowflake falls, it changes shape. That is why no two snowflakes are the same.

The shape of each snowflake is very important. Some shapes will make the snow strong, but others make the snow weak. Strong snow stays together well. But weak snow moves. A lot of weak snow may be an avalanche in the making.

*Every mountain in the world, such as Mount Superior in Utah, has layers of weak and ▶ strong snow in its snowpack.*

# What Is an Avalanche?

An avalanche is a big pile of snow that slides down a mountain slope. When the snow can no longer stick together, **gravity** (GRA-vih-tee) pulls it down. Two things are needed to start an avalanche. One is a slope covered with snow. The other is a trigger, or something that makes the snow move. An avalanche trigger can be wind, a skier, or even the sound of someone's voice.

To understand the possible danger of an avalanche, we must first look at the different layers of snow on the slope.

*Some avalanches are small. Others are very large and can tear down trees, boulders, and even houses.*

# Snow Layers

As snow falls and hits the ground, many layers build on top of one another. This makes a **snowpack** (SNOH-pak). We know that snowflakes change as they fall. But the snow continues to change even after it hits the ground. Snow can change because of the sun, the wind, or the temperature. When ice crystals are shaped in a way that makes it hard for the snow to stick together, a weak layer of snow is formed in the snowpack. A weak layer of snow will slide easily. The type of avalanche that happens depends on where this weak layer is found.

*Different weather conditions cause different layers of snow to form in a snowpack. Where these layers form and how strong they are is different in every snowpack.* ▶

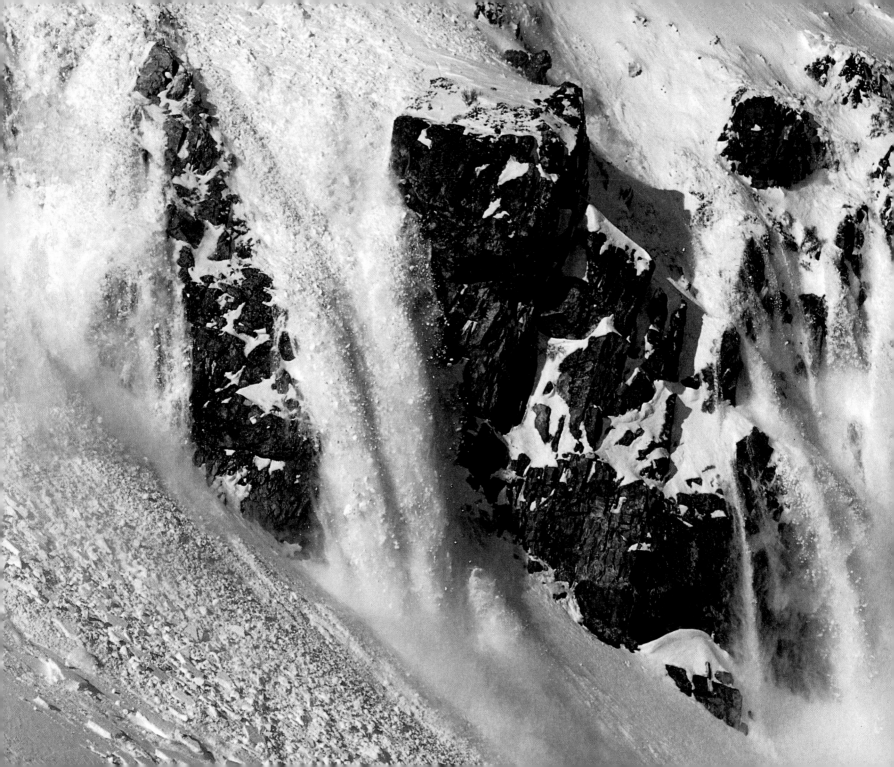

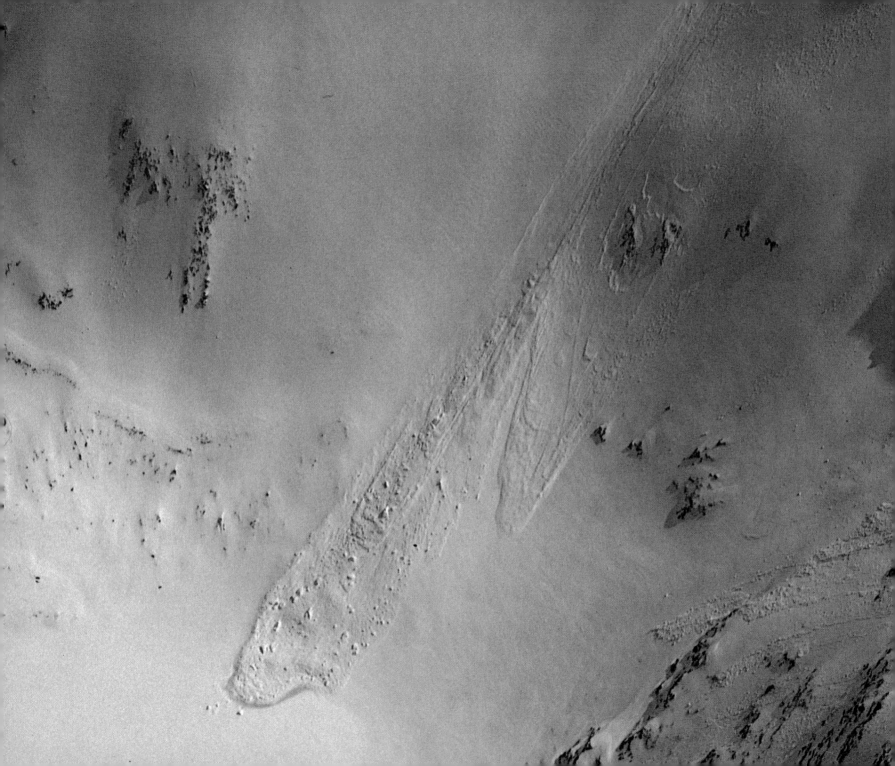

# Sluffs

A sluff is one type of avalanche. A sluff happens when the weak layer of snow is on the very top of a snowpack. Sluffs are not very dangerous because they don't carry a large amount of snow. The snow that they do carry is light and loose, like powder. Sluffs occur most often after a big snowstorm. The new snow piles on top of snow that is wet or icy. This smooth surface helps the new snow slide down easily. As the snow slides, it gathers more snow with it and spreads out in the shape of a big triangle.

◄ *This is the beginning of a sluff avalanche. See how it starts at one point and then spreads out? The sluff will continue to spread out at the bottom until the snow stops sliding.*

# Slab Avalanches

Another type of avalanche is called a slab avalanche. Slab avalanches can be much more dangerous than sluffs. That is because the weak layer of snow that causes the avalanche is buried deep in the snowpack. When it slides down the slope, all the snow that lies on top of it slides with it. The snow on top is called a slab, which is strong and hard. Slab avalanches carry huge amounts of snow and can move as fast as 200 miles per hour! They are so powerful that they take trees and rocks with them down the slope. As the slab rushes down, it heats up from the **friction** (FRIK-shun) and some of the snow melts. When it stops, the snow freezes again and becomes as hard as **concrete** (KON-kreet).

*Slab avalanches are often triggered by skiers who are skiing in the middle of the slab. This is very dangerous for the skiers.* ▶

# Avalanche Control

Millions of avalanches happen each year all over the world. But people aren't in danger unless they are in the way. When people ski or hike in an avalanche area, they are in danger. That is why many ski resorts do avalanche control. **Experts** (EK-sperts) at ski resorts make avalanches happen on purpose by shooting at snowpacks with guns. This removes weak snow, making the slopes free of avalanches and safe for people. This is done at night or in the morning, when nobody can get hurt.

But some people ski or hike in places where avalanches are not controlled. Because of this, thousands of people die each year in avalanches that they cause themselves.

◀ *Workers at ski areas do what they can to prevent avalanches from happening.*

15

# Finding Victims

When someone is buried under an avalanche, it's very important to find the person fast. That is because there is very little **oxygen** (AHK-sih-jin) for that person to breathe under the snow. After about twenty minutes, the oxygen usually runs out. Without oxygen, a person will die.

In 1968 Dr. John Lawton invented a beeper to help find buried avalanche victims. If someone is in an area where an avalanche might happen, he or she wears the beeper. If that person gets buried, the beeper sends out a **signal** (SIG-nul) so that others can find him or her. Then they can dig the avalanche victim out of the snow.

*It can take many people and a lot of time to dig victims out of an avalanche.* ▶

# Rescue Dogs

Avalanche rescue teams know that a victim may not have an avalanche beeper. So rescue teams use dogs to help find victims and dig them out of the snow. Many ski resorts have avalanche-dog programs that train dogs to find victims. This is done by teaching the dogs to find objects buried in the snow. A trainer will hide something with a human **scent** (SENT) on it, then use commands such as "Search!" or "Find 'em!" to tell the dogs to go to work. The dogs learn to work fast. The trainers know that the faster the dogs work, the better chance there is of saving a life.

◀ *When a rescue dog thinks she has found a person buried in the snow, she barks and starts to dig. This tells her human partners to start digging too.*

# Avalanche in Iceland

Sometimes an avalanche **threatens** (THREH-tunz) an entire town or city. This happened in Flateyri, Iceland, in October 1995. After a week of heavy snowfall, an avalanche warning was sent out. Flateyri has a long history of avalanches. The people there thought they knew which parts of town were safe. People in the dangerous areas moved to safer places in town. But the avalanche was bigger than anyone in the town had ever seen. It reached farther than any avalanche ever had before. By the next morning, 250,000 tons of snow covered Flateyri. Twenty people had been killed, and many homes were lost.

*Avalanches happen on mountains all around the world. This avalanche is on Karakoram Himalaya Mountain, in the country of Pakistan.* ▶

# Future Avalanche Protection

Many avalanche experts study snowpacks very closely. They do tests to find the weak layers of snow across a whole mountain range. Experts hope to understand how and why the snowpack changes. This could help them **predict** (pre-DIKT) when and where an avalanche may strike. It may also tell them what path the avalanche may take. But until avalanches can be predicted, towns like Flateyri must find ways to protect themselves. The people of Flateyri are building a wall 60 feet high that they hope will block future avalanches and keep people safe.

# Web Sites:

You can learn more about avalanches at this Web site:
http://www.pbs.org/wgbh/avalanche/elements.html

# Glossary

**concrete** (KON-kreet)  A hard, strong building material made by mixing cement with water, rocks, and gravel.

**crystal** (KRIS-tul)  A particle that forms when certain substances become solid, such as water becoming ice.

**expert** (EK-spert)  A person who knows a lot about a subject.

**friction** (FRIK-shun)  The rubbing of one thing against another.

**gravity** (GRA-vih-tee)  A natural force that causes objects to be attracted to each other.

**oxygen** (AHK-sih-jin)  A colorless gas that makes up part of the air we breathe.

**particle** (PAR-tih-kul)  A small piece of something.

**predict** (pre-DIKT)  To think and say something is going to happen before it happens.

**scent** (SENT)  A smell.

**signal** (SIG-nul)  A sound or other sign of warning.

**snowpack** (SNOH-pak)  The layers of snow that have built up on a slope.

**threaten** (THREH-tun)  The possibility of causing harm.

**vapor** (VAY-per)  The gas that is formed when a liquid heats up and evaporates.

# Index